Paul's Revelation:

The Gospel of Reconciliation

By Kenneth E. Hagin

Chapter 1
PAUL'S THREE PRINCIPLES

...I certify you, brethren, that the gospel which was preached of me is not after man.

For I neither received it of man, neither was I taught it, but by the revelation of Jesus Christ.

For ye have heard of my conversation in time past in the Jews' religion, how that beyond measure I persecuted the church of God, and wasted it:

And profited in the Jews' religion above many my equals in mine own nation, being more exceedingly zealous of the traditions of my fathers.

But when it pleased God, who separated me from my mother's womb, and called me by his grace,

To reveal his Son in me, that I might preach him among the heathen; immediately I conferred not with flesh and blood:

Neither went I up to Jerusalem to them which were apostles before me; but I went into Arabia, and returned again unto Damascus.

Then after three years I went up to Jerusalem to see Peter, and abode with him fifteen days.

But other of the apostles saw I none, save James the Lord's brother.

Now the things which I write unto you, behold, before God, I lie not.

Afterwards I came into the regions of Syria and Cilicia;

And was unknown by face unto the churches of Judaea which were in Christ:

But they had heard only, That he which persecuted us in times past now preacheth the faith which once he destroyed.

And they glorified God in me.

Then fourteen years after I went up again

to Jerusalem with Barnabas, and took Titus with me also.

And I went up by revelation, and communicated unto them that gospel which I preach among the Gentiles, but privately to them which were of reputation, lest by any means I should run, or had run, in vain.

— Galatians 1:11—2:2

In this message, I want to discuss God's revelation of Jesus Christ to the Apostle Paul. In this revelation, we see the supernatural element of Christianity in a light that the modern church never has seen.

Paul's revelation begins with Jesus' being made sin. It continues through the 40-day period from His crucifixion to His being seated at the right hand of Majesty on High. It deals with what Jesus did and what was done to Him during the three days and nights before He arose from the dead: How He carried His blood into the heavenly Holy of Holies, and how He eventually sat down at the right hand of the Father.

Paul's revelation deals with three major facts:

1. What God did for us in Christ in His great plan of redemption (or substitution).

2. What the Holy Spirit, through the Word, can do in us in the New Birth and in being filled with the Holy Spirit.

3. What Jesus is doing for us now at the right hand of the Father.

We will deal limitedly with the first two in this lesson. The third point is covered in my book *The Present-Day Ministry of Jesus Christ.*

Examining some phrases from our text, we find that Paul said, *"But I certify you, brethren, that the gospel which was preached of me is not after man. For I neither received it of man, neither was I taught it, but by the revelation of Jesus Christ."* (No man taught it to him. He heard no one preach it. He had not been one of the disciples who traveled with Jesus.)

Then in verse 17 Paul says, *"Neither went I up to Jerusalem to them which were apostles before me; but I went into Arabia, and returned again unto Damascus. Then after three years I went up to Jerusalem to see Peter, and abode with him fifteen days. But other of the apostles saw I none, save James the Lord's brother."*

Some have thought that Paul was in Arabia

three years; however, the Bible does not say how long he was in Arabia. It does say that three years after returning to Damascus from Arabia he went up to Jerusalem. No one knows how long he was in Arabia, but it was while he was there that he learned what he knew by revelation — thank God the Holy Spirit taught him.

We see that three years after he returned to Damascus, he went up to Jerusalem to see Peter and stayed with him 15 days. While there, he happened to see James, the Lord's brother.

The second chapter of Galatians begins with Paul's saying, *"Then fourteen years after I went up again to Jerusalem . . . And I went up by revelation . . . ."*

So we know that in 17 years, except for the 15 days he was with Peter, Paul had no contact with the other apostles. He did not know what they were preaching or teaching.

Fourteen years after he was with Peter, Paul states that when he finally did go up to Jerusalem, it was by revelation. That means the Spirit of God revealed to him that he should go. (It would be wonderful if we would do some things by revelation! The Holy Spirit is the same today, and if we will learn to listen to Him, He will reveal things to us.)

In Jerusalem, Paul shared the Gospel he preached among the Gentiles. The Church leaders in Jerusalem did not know what he was preaching, and he did not know what they were preaching. Paul had not followed or even known Jesus in the flesh as the rest of them had; he followed Him entirely by the Spirit. All Paul knew was what he had learned from the Holy Spirit.

In all of Paul's writings to the Church, you will find the three main principles of this revelation of Jesus Christ. Paul gives advice concerning local situations, greets certain people, etc., but primarily in all of his letters Paul deals with the three major facts we listed earlier. It is extremely important that we fully grasp these basic facts.

Let us look first at what God did for us *in Christ* in His great plan of redemption or substitution.

What Jesus did was not for Himself, but for us. He died as our Substitute — in your place and in my place. All He did is marked to our credit and belongs to us. God set it down to our account.

It was imperative that Satan's authority over man be broken, and Jesus did not arise from the dead until He had conquered the adversary and had broken Satan's dominion.

COLOSSIANS 1:12-14
12 Giving thanks unto the Father . . . .
13 Who hath delivered us from the power of darkness, and hath translated us into the kingdom of his dear Son:
14 In whom we have redemption through his blood, even the forgiveness of sins.

This is speaking of God and what He did for us through Christ. Notice that this Scripture does not promise us that God will deliver us *if* we are good and *if* we attempt to do better. I will tell you what He has done: In Christ Jesus, God already has wrought deliverance for everybody. He has delivered us out of Satan's authority. This text says, *"Who hath delivered us from the power of darkness . . . ."*

The Greek word translated as "power" in verse 13 means "authority." In that word "darkness" is everything Satan is. Satan and his kingdom are called darkness. God and His kingdom are called "light."

The Bible says that we are not children of darkness but of light. (See Ephesians 5:8; First Thessalonians 5:5; Second Corinthians 6:14.) Darkness refers to Satan's kingdom, and we are told that Jesus has delivered us out of Satan's authority.

This Scripture in Colossians also says God "translated" us into the kingdom of His dear Son. To "translate" means to take out of one place and put into another. We were taken out of Satan's kingdom and put into God's kingdom. We were taken out of Satan's family and put into God's family. This is the New Birth!

This is what happened when Jesus died and rose from the dead. It became a reality in our lives when we were born again and made new creatures in Jesus Christ.

We have our redemption! We are not *waiting* for it. Thank God we have it *now*. We are delivered *now* from the authority of darkness.

Every believer has been delivered out of Satan's authority and has been translated into the family of God! One believer is not more delivered than another. One person does not have more freedom than another. Some believers just know what belongs to them and they know how to take advantage of it better than others. But, thank God, this freedom belongs to everyone, and if we would just listen to the Word of God, we could enjoy the reality of what is ours. Satan has no more dominion over us!

ROMANS 6:14
14 For sin shall not have dominion over you: for ye are not under the law, but under grace.

Another translation reads, "For sin shall not lord it over you . . . ." If anything has dominion over you, it is "lording it over you." Sin and Satan are synonymous terms. Satan and sin shall not have dominion over you. Why not? Because, thank God, we have a new Lord: the Lord Jesus Christ. He is our Lord — not Satan.

Satan shall not lord it over us. *Satan has no more dominion over the believer than Pharaoh had over the Children of Israel after they had crossed the Red Sea*. When Pharaoh's hosts decided to pursue the Children of Israel across the Red Sea to recapture them, the waters came together upon them, and they were drowned. Israel was forever free from Pharaoh! He had no more authority over them!

Since Satan has no authority or dominion over you, he cannot put sickness and disease on you without your consent. Sickness and disease are of Satan and his kingdom; they do not come from heaven. There is neither sickness nor disease in heaven. It is not the will of God for Christians to be ill. The Lord Jesus Christ Himself told us in what we call the Lord's Prayer to pray, "Thy will be done on earth as it is in heaven." And we know there is no sickness or disease in heaven.

As we saw, Satan cannot possibly put sickness and disease on you without consent. If he did, your consent may have been born of ignorance, but it was still consent. You may not have known how to keep Satan from afflicting you, or you may not have known how to take advantage of what belongs to you. Nevertheless, you still consented; otherwise, Satan could not have afflicted you.

JAMES 4:7
7 Submit yourselves therefore to God. Resist the devil, and he will flee from you.

There is no need for you to have trouble with the devil. Satan is conquered as far as you're concerned, because Jesus defeated Satan! He did it for you. *His* victory is *your* victory! The Bible says to resist the devil and he will flee from you. It doesn't say he *might* do it; it says he *will* do it. He *will* flee from you. (If he doesn't, you didn't resist him.)

The trouble with some people is that they have been pals with the devil. Dr. A. B. Simpson, founder of the Christian Missionary Alliance, said, "There are many fine Christian saints who are actually carrying a demon around with them in their body in the form of sickness and disease and petting him when they should have been casting him out!"

Smith Wigglesworth related how he was standing on a street corner in England waiting for a bus. A woman came out of a nearby apartment building to catch the same bus. A little dog followed her. She said to the little dog, "Now, dear, you can't go. You are going to have to go back." The little dog rubbed up against her ankles and wagged his tail. She said, "Now, honey, you can't go. You have to go back." He just rubbed all the more, wagging his tail.

Then the bus drove up and that woman stomped her foot and shouted, "Get!" That little dog stuck his tail between his legs and took off. Wigglesworth said he hollered out loud, "That's what you have to do to the devil!" Thank God for his boldness.

That is exactly what you have to do! The devil will take all of that "honey" business you want to give him. He will buddy up with you and rub up against you as long as you let him. But if you will put your foot down and say, "Get — in the name of Jesus Christ!" he will take off just as that little pup did.

Satan is not only conquered, but God has made us a new creature over whom Satan has no dominion whatsoever.

Remember, each of us is an individual member of the Body of Christ. We are His Body. Each of us has had the same New Birth. Each of us, individually, is a new creation. And all of us *together* make up a new creation — the Body of Christ. He is the Head; we are the Body.

The Body of Christ is in this earth. Satan is the god of this world (2 Cor. 4:4), but he does not have authority over the Body of Christ. Jesus said that the gates of hell shall not prevail against the Church (Matt. 16:18). But remember, the Church is not a building. The Church is not an organization. The Church is you and me. *The gates of hell shall not prevail against you and me!*

Satan has no dominion over the Church. If Satan had any dominion at all, even over the toenail of the little toe, he would have dominion over a part of the Body of Christ. I want to tell you that Satan has no authority, no dominion whatsoever, over any part, even the least member of the Body of Christ.

Even the least member of the Body of Christ has dominion over Satan!

EPHESIANS 1:15-23

15 Wherefore I also, after I heard of your faith in the Lord Jesus, and love unto all the saints,

16 Cease not to give thanks for you, making mention of you in my prayers,

17 That the God of our Lord Jesus Christ, the Father of glory, may give unto you the spirit of wisdom and revelation in the knowledge of him:

18 The eyes of your understanding being enlightened; that ye may know what is the hope of his calling, and what the riches of the glory of his inheritance in the saints,

19 And what is the exceeding greatness of his power

to usward who believe, according to the working of his mighty power,

20 Which he wrought in Christ, when he raised him from the dead, and set him at his own right hand in the heavenly places,

21 Far above all principality, and power, and might, and dominion, and every name that is named, not only in this world, but also in that which is to come:

22 And hath put all things under his feet, and gave him to be the head over all things to the church,

23 Which is his body, the fulness of him that filleth all in all.

Notice Paul wanted the eyes of their understanding to be enlightened. One of the things, among others, he wanted the Ephesians to see was that God has put all things under Christ's feet. God has given Christ to be the Head over all things to the Church, which is His Body. We are members of that Body.

When the Word states that everything is under Christ's feet, it does not refer to the literal feet of the Lord Jesus when He was here on the earth.

Christ is the Head; His Body is the Church. The "feet" are in the Body. All things have been put under His feet — under the Church.

Some say, "I guess I'm just the little toe."
Well, that's a part of the feet, and everything's
still beneath you!

Chapter 2
THE TRUE GOSPEL

Notice that after Jesus arose from the dead, He said, "...*All power* [or authority] *is given unto me in heaven and in earth*" (Matt. 28:18).

Jesus immediately took the authority given to Him in the earth and delegated it to His Body. (Actually, the only way He could have authority on the earth — He's not here — is through His Body.)

He said to us, "...*Go ye into all the world, and preach the gospel* [good news] *to every creature*" (Mark 16:15). What is this good news He wanted us to go tell? We've never really preached the Gospel yet. We've preached *a* gospel, but not *the* Gospel. When you discover what the Gospel really is, it may come as a great shock to you. It shocked me when I first discovered it!

This happened many years ago while I was preaching a meeting in California. One day I was alone in the church, praying and studying. I was sitting up on the platform, reading. I had my Bible open to Second Corinthians 5, and as

I read, the 17th and 18th verses leaped off that page.

What I read shocked me so much that I jumped out of the chair — I must have jumped three feet! My Bible went sailing one way and another book I had in my lap went sailing another way.

I said to myself, *No, no, no, I didn't read that right! No, it didn't say what I thought it did!* I was trembling.

I picked up my Bible and read it again. I thought, *No, I can't accept that — but it's there!* Here is what I read:

2 CORINTHIANS 5:17,18
17 Therefore if any man be in Christ, he is a new creature: old things are passed away; behold, all things are become new.
18 And all things are of God, who hath reconciled us to himself by Jesus Christ, and HATH GIVEN TO US THE MINISTRY OF RECONCILIATION.

Not only did God through Jesus defeat Satan, but God has made us new creations who have authority over Satan. He has no authority over us. We are new creatures. Old things are passed away. All things are become new.

And all of these things are of God, who has reconciled us to Himself by Jesus Christ. And He has given us the ministry of reconciliation. But what is the ministry of reconciliation?

2 CORINTHIANS 5:19
19 To wit, that God was in Christ, reconciling the world unto himself, not imputing their trespasses unto them; and hath committed unto us the word of reconciliation.

Let us read that 19th verse again from *The Amplified Bible:* "It was God (personally present) in Christ, reconciling and restoring the world to favor with Himself, not counting up and holding against [men] their trespasses [but cancelling them]; and committing to us the message of reconciliation — of the restoration to favor."

He has committed this message of reconciliation and of restoring to favor to us. He doesn't want us to go tell sinners that if they will be good and cry half the night, or if they will do a penance half a year, He might eventually have mercy on them and do something for them. No!

He wants us to tell them that God Almighty

*has already cancelled out their debt. He is not
holding one thing against them!*

Someone said, "Well, if He isn't, then they
will all go to heaven." No, they are still children
of the devil. They must become children of God
in order to enter heaven.

God *has* cancelled out their trespasses; He
is not "going to." Can't you see we have never
told them that good news? Instead, believers
have gone out and have beaten poor old sinners
over the head and then wondered why they quit
coming to church. An old hog would have
enough sense to quit coming if someone took
a ball bat and beat his head every time he came
up to eat!

You do not find anywhere in the Bible where
God told us to go out and club the sinner, yet
people think you are supposed to do that. No,
the sinner is *already* under conviction.

And may God have mercy on some preach-
ers and pastors who have preached to saints as
if they were sinners. They think they are supposed to *keep* them under conviction and *keep*
them praying in the altar. It is good for people
to pray, but you don't have to beat them over
the head to get them to pray! Much of the time

these people don't know whether they are saved or not. They go to church and go home condemned. They want to hear the truth. *I am convinced that if the full truth were given, people would run over themselves getting to church.*

Let's continue reading verse 20 from *The Amplified Bible:* "So we are Christ's ambassadors, God making His appeal as it were through us. We [as Christ's personal representatives] beg you for His sake to lay hold of the divine favor [now offered you] and be reconciled to God."

Just come and lay hold of it! Just come and take it! Don't come and cry half the night. Don't come and see if you can talk God into the idea of doing something for you. He was personally present in Christ already doing something for you. Come and "lay hold of the divine favor [now offered you] and *be reconciled to God."*

That is the Gospel! That is the Good News!

Paul says in Romans 1:16, *"For I am not ashamed of the gospel of Christ: for it is the power of God unto salvation to every one that believeth; to the Jew first, and also to the Greek."*

The Hebrew and Greek words for salvation imply the ideas of deliverance, safety, preservation, healing, and soundness.

Do you see that when your debt of sin is cancelled, you can be healed? Sickness came as a result of sin — not necessarily your sin, but Adam's sin in the beginning. We all fall heir to it. But see now what has happened. Paul said, *"For I am not ashamed of the gospel of Christ, for it is the power...."*

What is the power? *The Gospel is the power!* It is *"the power of God unto salvation."* The Gospel is the power unto deliverance, safety, preservation, healing, and soundness. (This refers to both spiritual and physical healing and soundness.)

Now we can understand something in the following passage from the Book of Acts. The Bible says that Barnabas and Paul went to Lystra and Derbe, cities of Lycaonia and the surrounding regions,

ACTS 14:7-10

7 And there they preached the gospel.

8 And there sat a certain man at Lystra, impotent in his feet, being a cripple from his mother's womb, who never had walked:

9 The same heard Paul speak: who stedfastly beholding him, and perceiving that he had faith to be healed,
10 Said with a loud voice, Stand upright on thy feet. And he leaped and walked.

What did that — some power Paul had because he was an apostle? No, Paul didn't heal that man. It says the man had faith to be healed. Where did he get the faith? Verse seven tells us, *"And there they preached the gospel."*

That man heard Paul tell them *the Gospel* — the Good News. What was Paul saying? He was telling him that God was personally present in Christ Jesus, restoring the world (that included this crippled man) into favor with Himself, not counting up or holding against him his sins, but cancelling them out. And that now, because He had cancelled them out, Satan had no more authority to rule over him with sickness and disease, but he could be delivered from the penalty and result of wrongdoing.

The crippled man heard Paul and believed his message. Paul looked toward him and perceived that he had received the message and had faith from hearing the Word. So he said, *"Stand upright on thy feet."* And the man leaped and walked. It was just that simple.

Let's go back now to Mark 16, where Jesus told us, *"Go ye into all the world, and preach the gospel."* We have established what the Gospel is. Jesus went on to say, *". . .preach the gospel to every creature. He that believeth and is baptized shall be saved; but he that believeth not shall be damned"* (vv. 15,16).

Sinners are invited simply to come lay hold of this favor so freely offered. Of course, if a man rejects it, it won't do him any good. He will remain a child of the devil, and he will have to go to hell when he dies. But if he accepts it, he will be born again and become a child of God!

Chapter 3
PARADISE REGAINED

And these signs shall follow them that believe; In my name shall they cast out devils; they shall speak with new tongues;

They shall take up serpents; and if they drink any deadly thing, it shall not hurt them; they shall lay hands on the sick, and they shall recover.

— Mark 16:17,18

Jesus said, *"These signs shall follow them that believe...."* Follow the apostles? No. Follow the Early Church? No. Follow certain people, such as evangelists, prophets, pastors, or teachers? No, He said they shall follow *"them that believe."* These signs will follow those who believe, those who accept, this Gospel.

Jesus mentioned five signs. All of these five signs (which are now restored to the believer) originally were lost as a result of the curse on man and the earth.

First, God made the world and the fullness thereof, and He gave Adam dominion over all the works of His hands. God made Adam the god of this world. Adam, however, committed high treason and sold out to Satan. Then Satan and evil spirits began to dominate the earth.

But now when you hear and believe the Gospel, something happens. Believers exercise authority over the devil in Jesus' Name.

1. *"In my name shall they cast out devils."*

That simply states that every believer has authority over the devil. *"Resist the devil and he will flee from you."* You can put him on the run. If the devil invades your home, cast him out. You have authority over evil spirits.

The devil is the one who stops money from coming to you. The money you need is down here on earth. God is not a counterfeiter. He is not going to counterfeit $5 or $10 bills and rain them down from heaven! That would be wrong. It is not God who is withholding from you; it is the devil.

The Lord told me several years ago as I was complaining about needing money, "Well, I can't do anything about it. It is up to you. You command it to come in Jesus' Name. Use the authority. Say, 'In Jesus' Name, Satan, take your hands off my money!'

"You even can speak to the angels," He told

me, "and they will go to work for you, because
they are ministering spirits sent to minister for
those who are the heirs of salvation."

HEBREWS 1:14
**14 Are they not all ministering spirits, sent forth to
minister for them who shall be heirs of salvation?**

God is trying His best to get us to see the
truth, rise up in the light of that which is ours,
and go forth in power. Many are waiting for
God to do something. He is not going to do
anything. He already has done all He is going
to do about the situation.

"THEY will cast out devils," Jesus said.

2. *"They shall speak with new tongues...."*

What does the Bible say about speaking in
tongues?

1 CORINTHIANS 14:2
**2 For he that speaketh in an unknown tongue
speaketh not unto men, but unto God: for no man
understandeth him; howbeit in the Spirit he speaketh
mysteries.**

Weymouth's translation of that verse says,
"He talks divine secrets."

1 CORINTHIANS 14:14
14 For if I pray in an unknown tongue, MY SPIRIT
PRAYETH, but my understanding is unfruitful.

Let's go back to the beginning. Before
Adam sinned, he walked and talked with God.
But when God came down into the Garden of
Eden, Adam and Eve didn't see Him in the
same way they saw one another, because God
is a Spirit. God didn't just walk up to Adam
like a man would and then go for a walk with
him.

Adam did not see God with his physical
eyes. He did not talk to God out of his natural
mind. Nor did he contact God with a physical
hand. But he *did* walk and talk with God.
Adam, the real man, the inner man, the spirit,
walked and talked with God.

You see, it was when man sinned that his
body began to dominate him. Before that, his
spirit — the real man, the inner man — domi-
nated him. Adam and Eve had no clothes on,
and they didn't even know it. They didn't know
evil or sin. And God came down in the cool of
the day, and He and Adam walked and talked
secrets. But man lost that fellowship because

of the curse which resulted from sin.

In the Gospel, however, man is reconciled — restored — to God, and one of the signs that Jesus said would follow the believer is that he will speak with new tongues!

Many prayers prayed out of men's heads don't reach any higher than the ceiling. But you can be sure of one thing: If any man speaks in an unknown tongue, he speaks not unto men, but unto God.

God has devised a supernatural, divine means of communication with Himself whereby we once again can have that walk with God. *"Howbeit in the spirit he speaketh mysteries."* Once again man speaks divine secrets!

No, we are not "going up" to walk with Him. We walk with Him now. We talk with Him now.

Paul said, *"For if I pray in an unknown tongue, MY SPIRIT PRAYETH."* Jesus said, *"GOD IS A SPIRIT: and they that worship him MUST WORSHIP HIM IN SPIRIT and in truth"* (John 4:24). When I am talking in tongues, my spirit is in direct contact with the Father of spirits, God.

Some have said, "I don't see any need of it." If they understood the Gospel and the reconciliation of man's spirit to God, they could see it.

3. *"They shall take up serpents."*

This does not mean that believers are to handle snakes just to prove something! It refers to being accidentally bitten, as Paul was on the Island of Melita, when that viper came out of the fire and fastened itself to his hand (Acts 28). Paul just shook it off because, through the Gospel, we are redeemed.

The serpent is in the condition it is in today because of the curse put on it. When Satan is eliminated from the earth, there shall be nothing here to hurt or destroy us. But we have power and authority *now* over Satan. Satan is called a snake, too. This literally means that if a snake bites you, you can shake it off, but it also means that you have spiritual authority over that old snake, that old serpent, Satan.

4. *"And if they drink any deadly thing, it shall not hurt them."*

All that God made in the beginning was good. There was nothing to hurt or destroy man. All that changed when the devil became the god of this world. It need not affect us, though, because although we are in the world, we are not of the world. We have the authority!

5. *"They shall lay hands on the sick, and they shall recover."*

This means exactly what it says. Every believer has the authority to lay hands on the sick and expect them to recover! Jesus said, *"They SHALL recover."*

Jesus said that all five of these signs shall follow believers. And all of those signs, now restored to believers, originated in response to the curse.

GALATIANS 3:13
13 Christ hath redeemed us from the curse of the law, being made a curse for us: for it is written, Cursed is every one that hangeth on a tree.

Christ has redeemed us from the curse! We are not under the curse! That is what He did for us. That is what belongs to us.

It is ours *now*. We don't have to cry, pray, and fast three weeks and promise that we'll do better if He'll just give it to us. It all goes with the Gospel! It is just as much ours as our hands and feet are. All we have to do is start using it. The hour is *now*.

HEBREWS 1:1-14

1   God, who at sundry times and in divers manners spake in time past unto the fathers by the prophets,

2   Hath in these last days spoken unto us by his Son, whom he hath appointed heir of all things, by whom also he made the worlds;

3   Who being the brightness of his glory, and the express image of his person, and upholding all things by the word of his power, when he had by himself purged our sins, sat down on the right hand of the Majesty on high;

4   Being made so much better than the angels, as he hath by inheritance obtained a more excellent name than they.

5   For unto which of the angels said he at any time, Thou art my son, this day have I begotten thee? And again, I will be to him a Father, and he shall be to me a Son?

6   And again, when he bringeth in the first begotten into the world, he saith, And let all the angels of God worship him.

7   And of the angels he saith, Who maketh his angels spirits, and his ministers a flame of fire.

8   But unto the Son he saith, Thy throne, O God, is for ever and ever: a sceptre of righteousness is the sceptre of thy kingdom.

9   Thou hast loved righteousness, and hated iniquity; therefore God, even thy God, hath anointed thee with

the oil of gladness above thy fellows.

10 And, Thou, Lord, in the beginning hast laid the foundation of the earth; and the heavens are the works of thine hands:

11 They shall perish; but thou remainest; and they all shall wax old as doth a garment;

12 And as a vesture shalt thou fold them up, and they shall be changed: but thou art the same, and thy years shall not fail.

13 But to which of the angels said he at any time, Sit on my right hand, until I make thine enemies thy footstool?

14 Are they not all ministering spirits, sent forth to minister for them who shall be heirs of salvation?

Jesus is now seated on the right hand of God. We are expecting Him to come back. But I want to ask you a question: How long is Christ going to sit there in heaven?

The answer is found in verse 13: "...*until I make thine enemies thy footstool.*"

The only way God is going to overcome the enemy is through the Body of Christ, the Church. The last enemy to be put under foot by Jesus Christ is death itself (1 Cor. 15:26).